The Invisible Woman...

The Lonely World of Black Women in America—a Guide to Coping and Hoping

Evelyn Case

Copyright©2018 All rights reserved.
All rights reserved. This book may not be copied in print, electronically, in part or in whole without expressed written consent of the author.

Published by Love-LovePublishing, Madison, WI
ISBN: 978-0-9973200-3-9
Library of Congress Control Number: (pending)
The Invisible Woman: *The Lonely World of Black Women in America—a Guide to Coping and Hoping*
Evelyn Case
Available formats: eBook | Paperback distribution

Dedication

...to Black Woman

Contents

Chapter One: Perspective...........................1
Chapter Two: Interracial Dating................26
Chapter Three: Our Lives.......................33
Chapter Four: Solutions.........................35
Afterword: Finding Love........................39

Chapter One: Perspective

Putting my life and the lives of millions of Black women into words is no easy feat, especially in a country where we're often painted with the same brush, notorious for what Americans perceive as the "in your face" attitude of Black women, who are often demonized in the media as too loud, too feisty, violent or argumentative. Like other human beings, our attitudes are often a reflection of our social backgrounds, families, upbringing and economic situations. It is because of the many negative perceptions Black women endure, when pushed into a corner that we come out swinging. Because of this, the perception has been that if you cut a Black woman, we're not going to bleed. It's okay to disappoint us, mistreat us, or introduce situations into our lives that is beneath what one would consider the norm for other women.

However, it is my contention that Black women not only bleed when cut, we *hemorrhage*. Despite the stereotypes we are gentle loving mothers and women quietly, bravely, enduring a life of crippling inescapable loneliness, a side of us the world doesn't [or chooses not to] see. While there are many types of Black women who may or may not identify with this analysis, today, I write about one group of Black woman in particular...*the Invisible Woman*... Black women who will live the duration of their lives without a husband or significant other. The prognosis is grim, but fear not, there is light at the end of the tunnel.

I don't quite understand how we arrived at this point in history. How or why this generation of Black women must face the possibility of spending the rest of our lives alone. Growing up, it certainly wasn't a question I ever thought I would have to ask, or a situation I ever thought I would have to face. Boys were ever present, asking me out on dates. And occasionally, men who had no business asking for my telephone number, often approached. Back then, I would blow them off without a second thought. When we're young we're practically beating men off with a stick, and have no idea that the older we get, the fewer prospects we'll have out there waiting for us. There are several reasons for that, some of which will be addressed later.

I live in Middle America. Right here in the Midwest, in the state of Wisconsin in the mid-sized city of Madison. Nineteen years ago, I lived in one of the biggest cities in the country, Chicago, IL. I left the city because of the growing violence, and the daily and often savage attacks on our children. I am a mother. My children were toddlers when I moved away, packing our bags one cold winter day on New Year's Eve, driving two and a half hours away to my quiet new life. Madison was a dream and an excellent place to raise children. The schools were so much better, providing an environment where my children could actually learn without the distraction of Black on Black violence and overcrowded classrooms, though much to deal with in terms of implicit biases while going to predominately white schools. But that's a different story for another day. I jumped right in to my new life, taking an office job, working a nine-to-five in order to get on my feet while working on my writing career. At the time, I had no idea what awaited me as a woman, which was fifteen long years of singlehood.

My singlehood started in 1998. It's 2012, and I haven't been kissed in more than a decade.

Those are painful words to write. I no longer know what it feels like to have someone hold my hand, to share a secret, or my accomplishments with. Even as a mother with children, I can no longer remember what it is like to make love. That is how long it has been. I was twenty-three when I became single, and thirty-eight when I wrote this book. I needed to vent. I needed someone to care.

It's a little embarrassing, and I used to think something was wrong with me. Why am I not dating? Why haven't I found a boyfriend? Why aren't men interested in me? Terribly clichéd questions single desperate women often ask when faced with finding a significant other. Society doesn't help much either. People will often attempt to invalidate our feelings because our single-hood as Black women, makes them uncomfortable. They assume something must be wrong with us [single Black women], and not with society. People chalk it up to single Black women being ugly, overweight, uneducated, having personality issues, or looking for the wrong guy. In other words, our singlehood is our fault. Black women have shouldered the blame singlehandedly for as long as I can remember. Especially when talking to Black men. In fact, there are thousands of videos on the Google video-sharing web site YouTube, uploaded by Black men stating various reasons why they hate or will never date a Black woman, and numerous counter-videos from Black women who either defend or express their obvious hurt. The videos are not for the weak-stomached, and reflect the rising trend of intra-racism within the Black community.

In Wisconsin, the community I moved to was very diverse, which was nice. However, the novelty of living in a diverse community had its impact on the Black community, in that it provided Black men proximity to the white community and an opportunity to date outside of their race. Many took advantage of that opportunity, choosing to marry or date outside of their race exclusively, while showing little to no interest in dating Black women. It was a bit of a culture shock. This isn't to say that I am against interracial dating. In fact, I am _for_ interracial dating. For example, marriages between Black men and White women indicates the progress we've made in America in terms of race. Now that Black men have the right to openly date and marry whomever they love, regardless of color, we are seeing a reflection of this represented throughout our culture in many positive ways. For the most part, Black men marry interracially for love and happiness, but there are some, who have been very vocal and very anti-Black woman in their pursuit of white women. These men reflect a common mindset against Black women. For example, take comments by Hollywood actor Wesley Snipes in a 1997 *Ebony Magazine* article written by Ebony Contributor, Lynn Norment:

'"Brothers who are very, very successful, or who have become somewhat successful, usually it's been at a great expense, unseen by the camera's eye….He doesn't want to come home to someone who's going to be mean and aggravating and unkind and who is going to be `please me, please me.' He doesn't want to come home to that. He doesn't want to come home to have a fight with someone who is supposed to be his helpmate. So it's very natural that he's going to turn to some place that's more compassionate…. You've worked hard and you deserve to come home to comforting. And usually a man who has that will appreciate it. Because I've never known one cat, all those cats I've hung out with and still hang out with, who found something that they really, really like and didn't go back to it. They all go back. It's very simple."

'When asked for clarification, Snipes emphasizes that he is not saying that a Black woman cannot be that type of woman a man wants to come home to. "Not at all," he declares. "Absolutely not. That's the point. I want to come home and I don't want to argue. I want to be pleasing, but if I ask you to get me a glass of water, you're going to say, `Them days is over.' please. Come on," Wesley says. "A man likes that. I don't know why. It's been that way forever. It makes him proud, you know, like when the guys come over and your lady comes out with a tray of food and says `I made this up for you.' And the guys are like, `Oh man, you've got a great woman.' And the man says, `Yeah, I do.' A man will appreciate it when you're kind and when you're nice."

'...Continuing with his openness, Snipes says he's had his heart broken more than once, and at times by Black women. "Most definitely. Most definitely," he says.'

It seems that Wesley Snipes is saying that he is choosing to overlook Black women because he has reached a point in his life where he has attained success, and deserves to have what he considers more than Black women have to offer because we are not comforting or compassionate enough, we are mean, aggravating, unkind, unhelpful, unsupportive, and unpleasing. Millions of Black women took offense to the comments made by Wesley Snipes and quietly boycotted his movies ever since. Black women were very hurt by his words. Most Black women are not angry about interracial dating, but are offended that some Black men feel that dating women of other races is a step up from dating Black women. For some, the subject matter of this book may come as a surprise, but for many Black women, this has been our experience.

Common reasons <u>I've been told</u> why Black women are single:

- Black women only want to date thugs.

Just one anecdote, I recall having a disagreement with one young man who had given his reasons for not dating Black women, claiming Black women only wanted to date "thugs." After the argument, he decided that I was the exception to the rule and was simply projecting my preferences onto other Black women, viewing us through rose-colored glasses. I found it ironic, that a Black man would deign to stereotype anyone, much less another Black person.

- Black women are argumentative.

Black, women argue and scream more than women of other races, and men don't want to deal with them.

- Black women are artificial

Some men blame trends like perms and hair weave as the source of their discontent with Black women. Ironically, they get over their discontent quickly enough, when dating non-Black women with bleached hair, spray on tans, fake boobs, and hair weave, and face makeup that conceals their natural complexion.

- Black women have too many kids

Men don't want to date women with children or other "baggage".

- Black women are too overweight or physically unappealing in other ways, when compared to women of other races.

Some Black men claim that some women do a poor job of taking care of themselves. Or simply put, Black women aren't attractive to them.

- Had a bad experience with a Black woman

Some men swear <u>all</u> Black women off, based on bad personal experiences.

Black women also have reasons for being single, in which Black men are taken to task:

- Black men want to have their cake and eat it too.

i.e., Black men are notorious cheaters and womanizers. Some women are choosing not to date, unable to find a monogamous Black man.

- Lack of security

Black women want an employable Black man, with an education or even better, a good job.

- Black men are otherwise, unavailable

Too many Black men imprisoned or dead.

While Black women, seem to have a practical list of reasons as to why they have chosen not to date or pursue a relationship, Black men use their reasons as an excuse to distance themselves from Black women emotionally, particularly men who specifically chose to date non-Black women or choose to date multiple Black women at once.

Black women in overcrowded low-income urban areas fare better in terms of finding relationships, but deal with other issues prevalent in poor communities, such as domestic abuse, man-sharing (a Black man with two separate families, multiple children, and lives), and prison. This isn't to say that women in low-income neighborhoods can't have healthy relationships. There are many loving relationships in the Black community, especially among older couples, but those relationships are far outnumbered by single parent homes, single mothers, and single Black women. Black people in general, hate to read or even hear the numbers, because our issues in America have been reduced to racial and political stereotypes that have little to do with who we are. Take for example, the "70% of Black children are born out of wedlock" study. This study, which has turned into a widely disseminated stereotype about the makeup of Black families, was based on a 2006 study that documented the number of births that year.

Page six of a report in the Center for Disease Control's 2006 Census data, shows 70% of Black children out of 617,220 [Black] births that year, were born to Black mothers who were not married at the time that they gave birth (Source: United States Center for Disease Control 2006 Census data

(Source: http://www.cdc.gov/nchs/data/nvsr/nvsr56/nvsr56_07.pdf).

This report turned into a widely reported news item and stereotype that claimed that 70% of Black children were born out of wedlock, later transmuting to several "70% of Black women…" myths, since, including the most recent, which is that 70% of Black families did not have a man in the household. This may seem counter-intuitive to the point of my analysis with regard to the Invisible Black Woman, but I think it should be addressed.

Poverty's role in destroying Black Marriage:

What the report doesn't reveal is whether the parents married after the child's birth, be it the next day or a few years down the line. It merely reflects the marital status of the mother at the time that she gave birth or what was reported to the hospital by the mother. Particularly, **lower-income** Black women <u>will not report</u> their marital or relationship status in order to protect their economic situation, which may depend on government entitlement programs. Reporting an adult male or spouse in the household could lower those entitlements which are already limited and likely needed in a household where resources are scarce. Entitlement programs and benefits played a role in the decline of Black marriage since the 1960s, mostly among the poor, who relied on those social programs to get by. There is a huge disparity in marriage rates between middle-class and lower-income, with middle-class Black people having higher marriage rates. Middle-class Black people didn't rely on government programs and could marry without economic penalty. According to the 2001 article, *African American Marriage Patterns* by Douglas J. Besharov and Andrew West published by the *Hoover Press: Thernstrom*, the number of unmarried Black women over 40 rose 200% between 1950 and 1998, from 5% of the population to 15% of Black women. Black marriage declined dramatically when welfare was expanded to include Black mothers in the 1960s. Even then, the government understood that welfare discouraged marriage.

The decline in Black relationships and marriage started exclusively, in low-income areas as the result of welfare programs started by Franklin D. Roosevelt's *New Deal* program. Welfare was created for white women who had lost their husbands due to abandonment, desertion, or war, during a time when women relied on their spouses for financial support. However, Black women were already a part of the work force, were always expected to work, and therefore, excluded from receiving welfare benefits until the mid-1960s when laws changed to include Black people. This support led to plummeting marriage rates in the Black community. Welfare benefits were generally, designed to help the children of single mothers. The program involved social workers visiting the homes of single women to verify that a husband or boyfriend did not live in the household with the mother and children. Every item in the household had to be accounted for in the family's income. The family might have to justify how they could afford a new toaster, or a new TV, for example to prove that the family did not have additional income coming into the home, and to prove that the mother was in fact unmarried. Social workers would even check closets for male clothing. So many Black families, in need of support, chose not to marry and in some cases, lived separately in order to meet the requirements of welfare programs. It wasn't that Black men did not want to work. But salary disparities and discrimination often got in the way. Thus began the decline of Black marriage in low-income neighborhoods and families. The decline in marriage rates among lower income Black people had more to do with economics than Black people not falling in love or caring about each other. Unfortunately, Black men became even more disenfranchised, in society and in the home, creating a rift between Black men and women that exists today. This includes the 1996 welfare reform, that targeted Black men for financial support and often crippled them financially, leading to resentment between Black couples.

Over the years, scientists have tried

unsuccessfully, to address the decline in Black marriage, not realizing that while marriage was designed to improve the financial situation for white couples joined together in marriage, it tore Black families apart after the 1960s. This isn't to say that Black people needed welfare or other entitlements. There are as many middle-income or wealthy Black families with two parent homes, and a sound income. But for poorer families, marriage was a problem that got in the way of financial independence for Black women. Fortunately, laws have changed over the years, including incentives created by George W. Bush that rewarded families for staying together, but by then, it was too late. The damage had already been done. While white people make up majority of people on welfare, doubling the number of Black people who use welfare benefits, the perception that Black women rely on welfare, more than other racial groups has led to stereotypes that depict Black Women as undesirable.

Stereotypes:

Because information is so easily skewed, Black people realize they have to be careful about the how information is presented, since race-based science has always been used as a tool to hurt the image or to slander Black people, in order to justify historical racism and reinforce oppression. Black women have too often been on the receiving end of several unfortunate studies since the "70%" myth entered the mainstream. Stealing our beauty, robs us of our power as women. While any feminist will agree, we are more than just our looks, if you take that away from a woman, you rob her of the ability to find a potential mate. Black women are scrutinized over their looks more than women of any other racial group or tribe.

Take for example, the 2011 study by Satoshi Kanazawal, a Japanese scientist in the U.K., lecturer at the London School of Economics and evolutionary psychologist who claimed, Black women were less attractive than women of other races due to having more testosterone. His theory was made after a study in which White, Black, and Asian men and women were asked to rate the photos of people of different races and sexes. He claimed, Black women were found the least attractive in his report, *"Why are Black Women Rated Less Physically Attractive Than Other Women and Black Men are Rated Better Looking Than Other Men?"* (Source: *Psychology Today The*

Scientific Fundamentalist).

Kanazawal's study left much to be desired, as the number of participants in his study is currently unknown. The participants surveyed were also American, where the standard of beauty favors women with European features. Beauty is also highly subjective, one of many points the "scientist" failed to consider. In 2006, he also published a story that claimed that the poor health of Africans was the result of low I.Q., rather than poverty.

(Source: http://www.dailymail.co.uk/news/article-1388313/LSE-psychologist-Satoshi-Kanazawa-claims-Black-women-attractive.html).

Bear in mind, this is the same man who asserts "beautiful people are more intelligent", which if true, would probably explain his stupidity.

(Source:
http://www.psychologytoday.com/blog/the-scientific-fundamentalist/201012/beautiful-people-really-are-more-intelligent).

After Kanazawal's report, the London School of Economics conducted an internal investigation and found that Kanazawal had brought the prestigious school into "disrepute", a heavy charge, as colleagues in his field contested the science in Kanazawal's report as flawed. He was later barred by LSE from publishing in non-peer reviewed journals for a year, and stripped of teaching compulsory courses for the

remainder of 2011.
(Source: http://www.timeshighereducation.co.uk/story.asp?sectioncode=26&storycode=417449&c=1).

Kanazawal isn't the first, and certainly won't be the last pseudo-scientist to make claims based on race, of which, blacks are on the blunt end of the report. From the "Black people read slower because their eyes are bigger" to the study that claimed "Black people smell worse than other races because they have larger apocrine glands". When it comes to the Black community and science, the premise is that Black people are inherently flawed, so the science community is in constant pursuit of coming up with a solution to issues that begins with a flawed premise in the first place – one that is rooted in prejudice and bigotry. We are under attack physically, mentally and socially, so we spend our time defending ourselves and the good relationships that do exist in spite of the numbers and the declining marital rates and the Invisible Black Women destined to live out the remainder of their days alone if we continue along this path.

Racial stereotyping in America and abroad has made it nearly impossible for Black people to deal with internal problems honestly and openly for fear that our conversation will spin out into the stratosphere as fodder for racist dogma. What we need to do is look past the flaws of the world we live in, in order to deal with our issues.

Listening to YouTube videos, reading articles and anonymous online comments from people making derogatory comments about the appearance of Black women, left me wondering if I was in fact, unattractive to the opposite sex. Would it explain, why I had not been in a relationship for more than ten years? The reason why not one single man has ever asked me out on a date or for my telephone number? Why men of all races look through me and not at me, like I am the *invisible* woman?

I can't speak to anyone else's taste in women, but I have been told in passing that I am either pretty or attractive. But attraction comes down to more than ones actual appearance.

So why are Black women considered the least desired women in the world? Because *our men* don't desire us. Of course, they desire us sexually, or as a sexual tool for them to exploit and bear children with, but they do not value us emotionally or as equals, and publically, managed to disparage us in a number of ways.

There are Black men who do value their partners and are happily married, engaged, or otherwise dating, but these are also the same people who support or have remained silent when rap songs refer to Black women (i.e., their mothers and daughters) as bitches and whores. Rap music has been disseminated and enjoyed globally and set the tone for how the world perceives us, thus making it "okay" to discriminate and bash Black women. It is okay to call us ugly, or to call us whores or to call us 'ghetto' and frankly, we stand alone, and without protection like Venus Hottentots. White males, in history have always held White women up as the standard of beauty, even when they were sexist and chauvinist against them, they never sold them out as undesirable whores to be disrespected by men the world over. In fact, even when White women are depicted as "promiscuous" like the ladies of the television show, *Sex and the City*, they are written as likeable and relatable (hell, I love the show), whereas, a sexually active Black woman is just a welfare baby machine or a "hoe". I cannot recall, Black men uniting before the media, to stand up for us in my entire life. I cannot recall Black men standing up for Black women at any point in history – and I don't mean the civil rights movement, which intended equal rights for us all.

Rap music to Black women is what the burka has been to Middle Eastern women. It has been used to systematically subjugate and control the image and sexuality of Black women. Other seemingly harmless depictions of Black women include men like Tyler Perry or Martin Lawrence in drag, depicting us in an unflattering light.
Black women also shoulders some of the responsibility, particularly the ones who have supported rap music over the years.

Black men have enjoyed the exclusivity of having Black women to themselves, while Black women must compete not only with each other, for the limited number of available Black men, but also women of other races. Despite a few decades of complaining about Black men in literature, their unwillingness to provide, commit, and painful issues surrounding constant infidelity, we still held them up as an object of desire, intelligence, attractiveness, virility and sexual prowess while Black men play us down as unworthy bitches. When men of other races show an interest in Black women, the idea that is reinforced is that those men can only see us as a sexual object, and nothing more.

The reason Black women are single, is because Black men maintain control of our relationships. Black women submit because finding a suitable mate is not only difficult, but next to impossible. If I left my mentally unstable ex and the father of my children fourteen years ago, knowing I would never date again, would I have made the same decision? In hindsight, I'm certain I would, but I would have done more to prepare myself for my future as a perpetually single Black woman.

Some may ask, what's wrong with being single? Well, it becomes more difficult to survive on one income in our economy. It's even worse for single mothers. Single parent households can end up in a cycle of long-term dependency on the government. It's easy to point fingers and ask, why do women have children they can't afford in the first place. For one, being a mother is natural and a God given right. But I believe there are other reasons to avoid (if you can) raising children as a single parent.

Black marriage has been in steady decline since

the 1970s. According to the 2001 article, *African American Marriage Patterns* by Douglas J. Besharov and Andrew West published in the Hoover Press: Thernstrom, Black marriage has declined dramatically since the 1970s.

> *"Compared with white women, African American women are 25 percent less likely ever to have been married and about half as likely to be currently married. According to the Census Bureau's Current Population Survey (CPS), in 1998, about 29 percent of African American women aged fifteen and over were married with a spouse present, compared with about 55 percent of white women and 49 percent of Hispanic women. African American women are estimated to spend only half as long as white women married (22 percent vs. 44 percent of their lives). In the 1950s, after at least seventy years of rough parity, African American marriage rates began to fall behind white rates. In 1950, the percentages of white and African American women (aged fifteen and over) who were currently married*

were roughly the same, 67 percent and 64 percent, respectively. By 1998, the percentage of currently married white women had dropped by 13 percent to 58 percent. But the drop among African American women was 44 percent to 36 percent—more than three times larger. The declines for males were parallel, 12 percent for white men, 36 percent for African American men."

Perhaps Black women know on some level that they will never get married, and having children gives us a sense of purpose. My children have been companions to me over the past ten or so years, and as they move into adulthood, I imagine my life becoming a bit lonelier. I can almost hear the deafening silence of my empty nest and have even found myself fantasizing about having another baby someday. A baby to me is attainable, a significant other, not so much.

Chapter Two: Interracial Dating

I talked about Black men but haven't mentioned the possibility of finding love with men of other races. But do they find us attractive? The Kanazawal study isn't the only one that claims men of other races find Black women unattractive. Or better phrased, don't find Black women attractive. There was a study published on OKCupid.com (How Your Race Affects The Messages You Get), using data from the dating web site Match.com, which showed that when writing letters to members of the opposite sex, Black women were responded to less than women of other races. Here's what they found:

"Men don't write Black women back. Or rather, they write them back far less often than they should. Black women reply the most, yet get by far the fewest replies. Essentially every race—*including other blacks*—singles them out for the cold shoulder."

Black Women write back the most:

"Black women write back the most. Whether it's due to talkativeness, loneliness, or a sense of plain decency, Black women are by far the most likely to respond to a first contact attempt. In many cases, their response rate is one and a half times the average, and, overall, Black women reply about a quarter more often that other women."

In a poll shown in OKCupid's research, data showed that 22% of Black women prefer to date within their race compared to 11% of Black men.

There's good news, in terms of why men of other races don't respond to Black women. 40% of White men polled answered that they prefer to date within their own race. The numbers for Asian males were at 24%, and 18% of Latino men. So the fact that men of other races are not responding to Black women have less to do with whether or not they find Black women attractive or dateable, but is a reflection of their social views and willingness to date interracially. These men may not be inclined to date outside of their race with a woman of any ethnicity, so Black women shouldn't take it personally. It is also reasonable to assume that non-White foreigners in other countries, place high value on being White, so when seeking romance with someone outside of their country, they tend to look for White women instead of Black.

There are of course, other web sites like AfroRomance.com that cater to interracial dating. So as part of my research, I registered for the site, posted pictures on my new profile, and waited to see what would happen. Indeed, men of various ethnic backgrounds were interested, though mostly men of the Black and White variety.

I also used the search parameters provided to look for Asian and Latino men. Surprisingly, I found very few Latinos on AfroRomance.com who were interested in Black women. There were a total of six Asian males in the 18-70 year-old range who also showed in the results (nationally). One Asian (Chinese) male out of the six I found on the web site, happened to live in my city. His profile specifically stated that he was only interested in White women. Culturally, Asian males prefer women with White or milky complexions. In Asian societies, dark skin is associated with being poor, or a peasant, so Asians in China, Japan and occasionally South Korea, go through great pains to avoid looking dark to avoid being perceived as poor, or someone who performs manual labor out in the sun. Many (particularly the men) also avoid friendships with non-whites... especially Black Americans, since blacks are perceived to be at the bottom of the totem pole in western society, where Asians hope to assimilate.

In lieu of my research, I also read an article by a biracial half-Black half-Chinese woman (Blasian), living in China who wrote:

"Many Black women from all over the world contact me, often asking me if they will also have the chance to marry a Chinese man like I did if they move to China. However, more often than not I have to caution them that it's not quite that easy here. Although China is filled with the mixed couplings of White men/Chinese women, Chinese men/White women and Black men/Chinese women; when it come to Black women/Chinese men (BW/CM), the sightings are sadly few and far between.

"There are many reasons for this rarity in China. One comes from media stereotypes that portray Black women as difficult to control, oversexed, much larger in size and not attractive due to skin color and body shape. In return, Chinese men are portrayed as weak, shy men that would not be able satisfy a Black woman sexually. In addition to the media stereotypes, there is the traditional thinking and underlying prejudices that still exist in China regarding race mixing and the notion that a Chinese man's reputation and family must look good and be protected. Dating or marrying a Black woman would not look good in front of others and cause negative attention towards his family. However, marrying or dating a White woman seems to raise their status among their peers and is even celebrated by many."

(Source: http://www.echinacities.com/expat-corner/Black-women-chinese-men-where-s-the-love.html).

China has its own issues to deal with. Men in China outnumber women 30 to 1, so many of them will never marry. There is growing backlash against foreigners in China, as a result of Chinese women dating and marrying outside of their race, an issue similar to what Black women in America experience in terms of having fewer black men to date or marry.

What do we do as women, when men regard us as a source of embarrassment that would lower their social standing? Avoid shallow foreigner men! What can we do when Black men, see perceive Black women as easy to exploit because there are so few men available to us in our communities? Raise our standards by not compromising our values. Set the terms you desire in your relationships.

I can't change society or its views on race. Society has to want to change for the better, and that begins with how each person feels on the inside. Therefore, the views of foreigners shouldn't be internalized by Black women as their cultural beliefs have very little to do with *us* as women.

If you happen to meet someone who likes you as a person, his race shouldn't matter. Why limit yourselves to Black men, when they don't limit themselves to Black Women? You will hear throughout your life that men of other races don't have a genuine interest in Black women and the ones who do, will use us sexually. My advice is, no matter how lonely you feel, don't compromise your morals or self-respect for anyone. I have often found that men of other races, who do like Black women, tend to be more respectful than Black men. There is an openness and a desire to learn more about us, as they have already cast stereotypes and other social views aside in order to pursue relationships with Black women.

Men of other races *do* find Black women attractive, but they represent a special group of men. You just have to find them.

Chapter Three: Our Lives

I try not to project my insecurities and fears into my analysis of Black women and dating. But it's hard to separate myself from it at the same time. Especially when so many of my friends and family share the same pain.

One of my friends resorted to an arranged marriage to a Nigerian man. They are happily married for two years now. Another family member is dating several married men. My mother hasn't dated for probably 20+ years, and was single for most of my childhood, even though she was a career woman with a nice home and comfortable life. One of my closest friends is married to a younger man. He was six years her junior when they met (both of them in their 20s). She was a professional educated woman who had immigrated to the U.S. She made her needs clear to him from the beginning, and he became the kind of man she wanted to be with, they are happily married now, some thirteen years later. My sister married a man, almost twenty years her senior.

There is no one-size-fits-all scenario when it comes to our relationships. Just know yourself, and what you want out of life.

Chapter Four: Solutions?

Is there a solution to the *Invisible Black Woman* syndrome? Not really. Black people must first acknowledge that the problem exists before we can find a solution to our problems. There are many Black women and Black men who lead healthy normal lives, and have healthy happy relationships who would take exception to what I have written. There are also Black women who are suffering, but would prefer that I not speak for them. We are proud, and don't want to be perceived as weak, needy, lonely, or broken. We have it hard enough and would prefer not to deal with yet another label.

Parents in India choose the mates of their children, setting them up in arranged marriages. In fact, most marriages in India are through arranged marriages. Judaism teaches that one's mother has to be Jewish in order for the child to be considered Jewish. This practice strengthens the Jewish community and ensures that Jewish men marry Jewish women.

So can we begin our culture anew? Pair our children off in arranged marriages in order to give our girls a head start? Could something like this work in the Black community? *My son will marry your daughter if he stays on the right path, gets a good education and job?* If she does the same they will be together? Raise him with this goal in mind, that the two of them will be united someday. If he really likes her and sees her as someone he could be with for the rest of his life, will he pursue this relationship into adulthood?

So what are we to do to fix the broken family in the black community? What can we do to ensure that Black women will not be excluded from the game of love like the last kid standing after everyone has already picked their team? What can we do to ensure that as Black women, we are leading healthy, stress-free lives? It all begins with family life.

I believe sex is important, as well as restraint. I believe that having children without a marriage is fine, <u>as long as the parent is financially independent</u>. I would advise women to wait until they are financially stable before bringing children into the world without a husband. You have a life to live, so live it! Otherwise, tell your significant other to put a ring on it before you decide to have children together. It's important for you, your child, the community – and black women as a whole to take this important step.

Seek personal happiness. Use our free time to improve ourselves. I once saw a quote, which read, *"Love isn't something you find...love is something that finds you."*

My fifteen years of singlehood have not been in vain. I have written several books. I learned another language. I spend my time reading, painting, singing and growing a bountiful fruit and vegetable garden. I plan to travel in a few years, and I am saving accordingly. Whether I will have a man on my arm doesn't matter to me anymore. I wish things were different, I wish there was someone I could share my accomplishments with, someone I can lean on when I feel down. However, I have made peace with my life, and the fact that love may or may not happen. The truth is, I have attained happiness, from my accomplishments.

I would hope that Black women who read my analysis aren't discouraged, despite the sobering information before us. I am merely attempting to start some dialogue in the Black community about this serious situation.

Black women are beautiful, attractive, wonderful and smart. We have no control over how we are perceived, but as mothers, we *can* control the fate of our communities, by shaping and molding our sons to become the kind of men we would have wanted in our lives by encouraging them to love and cherish Black women. We can encourage our daughters to love themselves no matter what, and to be the very best they can be.

We cannot allow society or negative perceptions to dictate what will happen in our lives, much less our love lives. We must learn to tune out the noise, and move forward in order to achieve happiness. Even without a significant other, we can find happiness through focusing on our families and doing things that we love. Whether it's taking a class or finding a hobby. Find something in your life to feel passionate about to experience and bring a different type of joy into your life.

Afterword
Finding Love...

After throwing in the towel, giving up on relationships, and finding happiness within myself, I eventually found love a year after writing this book. I married in 2016. As the quote I mentioned before said, "Love isn't something you find, love is something that finds you." All of the things I did in order to find personal happiness in my life, were the very things my husband found most attractive in me as a person. The fact that I was an author, that I spoke Chinese, that I could sing, that I loved to garden, that I loved Kung Fu movies, and the mysteriousness of someone attractive being single for so long intrigued him. In fact, we met over our love of old school Kung Fu movies, added each other to Facebook, and stayed in touch. Two years later, he asked me out for a date, and the rest is history. He was local, and lived forty-minutes outside of my town. My only regret is that we met later in life. I would have loved if we had been able to raise my children together. They were teenagers when we met, and still trying to adjust to having a co-parent in our home, but they like him and get along with him and that's what matters most.

For the record, my husband is White. And when I wrote this book, it was 2012, I was single and had not yet met the man I was going to marry. It is now 2018 and we are going on five years together. I have been asked, if I was looking for someone who wasn't Black. For the record, we did not choose each other because of a specific interest in dating outside of our race. His last relationship, which lasted nine years, was to a white woman. And my last relationship, in 1998, was with a Black man. In the end, what does this tell you about what people have said about Black women and interracial relationships? What I loved about my husband was that he was very gentle with me, and careful about emotional and physical intimacy with someone who had not been in a relationship in fifteen years. He recognized very early on that I was afraid, and having the patience to deal with my fear, took his time. I recognized in him someone who cared about me as a person, someone who has nurtured me, even when I became ill early in our relationship. I guess the lesson in this, is love will happen when it happens…just be ready when it arrives. Don't look for a certain type of person, or a certain "race" in your search for a love. I believe we are destined for a certain person, and by cherry-picking certain qualities, you might find yourself on a path leading you away, rather than towards the person you are meant to be with.

The key to finding love is taking care of yourself and being a whole person. How can you find your soul mate when you haven't found yourself? Fear, self-loathing, anger, jealousy (towards other people) and the worse character-trait of all, **selfishness,** can hinder your blessings. Fear of being hurt prevented me from opening my heart. Fear of bringing someone into my life who could potentially hurt me and my children subconsciously prevented me from dating. Fear prevented me from doing many things…and that was fine. I needed to be in a comfortable place emotionally, spiritually, and physically before I could move forward and bring another human being into my life. When I was finally ready for love, it found me.

So before you embark on your journey to

happiness, ask yourself the following questions:

1. *What am I afraid of?*

Fear shows lack of faith. If you can honestly answer that you are afraid of nothing, then you are ready to love and to be loved.

2. *Who am I afraid of?*

If you can honestly answer that you are afraid of no one, then you are ready for love, and ready to be loved. This means you are ready for the challenges a relationship brings, and doing what it takes to make your relationship work. This does not mean compromising yourself and your values. You will recognize true love and what is worth fighting for when the time is right.

3. *Who do I hate?*

If you can honestly answer that you hate anyone (ex-boyfriends, ex-husbands, parent, family member, etc), then you are not ready for love. Resentment in your heart leaves less room for love. When you release anger and hatred, you are ready for love, and ready to be loved.

4. Who do I love?

If you can honestly answer that you genuinely love not only yourself, but that you love the family you nurture and protect even more than yourself, then you are ready for love, and ready to be loved.

When you love intensely, you will make choices and sacrifices for the betterment of everyone around you. A woman who is genuinely in love with herself and her family would never compromise herself or loved ones for men or people with selfish intentions. Women who love genuinely, do not hurt others. Their hearts are full, overflowing with compassion and selflessness. They do not covet what is not theirs (through envy, or by lusting after the husbands or boyfriends of someone else), they wear the armor of truth. A person who genuinely loves, lives honestly in every aspect of life.

The goodness we project is the goodness we receive from the Universe. Know that you are not invisible, and to those who are good and practice patience, good things will come.

About the Author

Evelyn Case is an author, entrepreneur, filmmaker, wife and mother.

www.ingramcontent.com/pod-product-compliance
Lightning Source LLC
Chambersburg PA
CBHW030459010526
44118CB00011B/1006